Ullie R Akerstrom

Poems by Ullie

Ullie R Akerstrom

Poems by Ullie

ISBN/EAN: 9783744711043

Printed in Europe, USA, Canada, Australia, Japan

Cover: Foto ©Thomas Meinert / pixelio.de

More available books at **www.hansebooks.com**

POEMS

BY

ULLIE.

[ULLIE R. AKERSTROM.]

CHICAGO, ILLS.
PUBLISHED BY THE AUTHOR.
1884.

Truly Yours
Ullie

To

My dear Mother,

MRS. ELIZABETH W. AKERSTROM.

This book is affectionately inscribed

by her daughter,

ULLIE.

INDEX.

DESCRIPTIVE.

HUMOROUS.

SENTIMENTAL.

RELIGIOUS.

DESCRIPTIVE.

The Miner's Protege.

WAL, you see it's a queer story, Missy,
  The little gal's none o' our kin;
But you bet when the old men go under
  She's the one who will handle our " tin."
My pard an' me's rough minin' fellers,
  We've got nary children nor wife;
But we love little yaller-haired Nellie,
  An' we'll rear her up right,—bet yer life.

How old ? Wal she's nigh eight I reckon,
  Five years since we brought her out here;
An' she was the cunninest baby
  We'd looked at for many a year.
Yer see 'twas the time the Apaches
  Broke out.   Blast the red imps o' sin!
The emigrant train crossed their trail, Miss,
  An' the Injuns they scooped 'em all in.

Yes, thar lay men, children an' wimmen;
  The red imps had raised all their ha'r;
We couldn't do nothin' to help 'em,
  So my pard an' me buried them thar.
Thar was one likely lookin' young cretur'
  Lyin' out from the rest of the heap;
She was dead like the rest—an' poor Nellie
  Was close by her side fast asleep.

Wal, 'twas nigh ninety miles to the settlement;
    Bill an' me turned the thing in our mind,
An' at last we concluded to keep her
    An' bring her up lovin' an kind.
We buried her poor dad an' mammy,
    Likewise all their unlucky mates,
An' we named her Nell, arter a sweetheart
    My pard had once, back in the States.

But the trouble we had with that young un
    Was somethin' quite funny to see;
Bill give her up for a mystery,
    Likewise she was too much for me.
Her durned duds, they wouldn't go on right,
    An' we cussed every button an' string;
But arter a spell we did better,
    When we once got the hang o' the thing.

An' she's growin' up pert-like an bloomin';
    We take her to work every day,
An' while Bill an' me's busy a minin'
    She'll sit on the rock pile an' play.
An' she's made better men of us both, Miss,
    We don't cuss now, nor go on no spree;
'Cause we're workin' an savin' for Nellie,
    The pride of my old pard an' me.

Right will E'er Prevail.

THOUGH this world of ours seems upside down,
  And under falsehood's sway,
I tell you, friends, there's coming soon
  A brighter, happier day.
There'll be a time when truth and love
  Will rule o'er hill and dale,
For a God of justice reigns above,
  And Right will e'er prevail.

Brothers, who trod the downward road
  Led on by fiendish rum,
But have broken loose from his fatal grasp,
  And the upward path begun—
Though shunned and doubted now by all,
  Do not o'er the past bewail :
You will yet regain your lost estate,
  For Right will e'er prevail.

Sisters, who strayed from virtue's peal,.
  But have now turned back again,
Press on ! for repentance, time and faith
  Will blot out the past's dark stain.
Take heart ! Work on in your self reform,
  Your efforts will *sure* avail;
For a God of Love doth watch above,
  And Right will e'er prevail.

Yea, earnest labor with heart and brain,
  And the help of God *will win*;
And honesty, temperance, virtue, still
  Will rise above crime and sin.
Then join hands in all the lands,
  And encourage the weak and frail;
Let them turn not back to sin's dark track,
  And may Truth and Right prevail.

Thoughts in a Church Yard.

YON mound by brightest flowers decked,
    Tells of a love not yet forgot;
Of thoughts that ever backward turn
    From busy life to this lone spot.

Like sea of living green outspread,
    By waving grass o'ergrown, *this* mound
Reminds us of the bright fresh fields,
    Where nature's free, rich gifts abound.

Yon sculptured marble, high and cold,
    A token seems of power and worth.
Not so—a poor, weak hope it shows,
    To be remembered on the earth.

Like blot upon a picture bright,
    This dark and bare unsodden spot
So drear, and from the rest apart,
    Seems by the whole wide world forgot.

Howe'er disguised beneath each mound,
    A hidden tenant ghastly lies,
A stark and mouldering, shrouded form
    Is buried deep from human eyes.

And so in life is man to man;
    We hear the jest, we see the smile,
Unheeding that the fair outside
    Conceals a sorrow all the while.

Some men are like the mound with flowers,
    Their lives seem full of bliss and light;
Yet, 'neath the brilliant, gay outside,
    Is hid some thought their joy to blight.

And others, like the marble high,
  Conceal their minds 'neath pride and gold.
But, ah! The rich man's haughty soul,
  At times is filled with woe untold.

And like the drear, unsodden spot,
  Is some poor, joyless human heart,
Which, filled with sad and gloomy thoughts,
  Seems fate-ordained to live apart.

Yes, 'neath the careless look, each heart
  Conceals some scar, some stab, some burn,
Or ruin of some cherished hope,
  To which the thoughts forever turn.

And like the graves, the covering bright
  Seems free from cloud as summer's sky;
Yet, like the graves, deep in each heart,
  The ashes of some image lie.

Never Dilly-dally.

WHAT e'er you have to carry, friend,
    Don't loiter by the road,
  Nor sit and wait for some one else
    To lighten up your load.
  If you intend to climb life's hill,
    Don't loiter in the valley;
  But warning take in time, my friend,
    And do not dilly-dally.

If you should love a lady fair
    And wish her for your bride;
  See that you speak your mind to her,
    Whatever may betide.

Keep other suitors in the rear:
  Perchance if you do tarry,
Some bolder heart will win her love,
  So, do not dilly-dally.

If you're in debt and have the means
  To pay your creditor;
Go while the money's in your hand,
  And send Debt from your door.
You'll feel a richer man, my friend,
  Your views with mine will tally;
You'll say with me, 'tis always best
  To never dilly-dally.

In short, whate'er you have to do,
  Do quickly and at once;
The man who stands and " hems and haws,"
  Is nothing but a dunce.
Life's hill is steep—if you would climb
  Don't loiter in the valley;
The winner in life's race is he
  Who does not dilly-dally.

Phantoms,

Y E phamtoms of the buried past,
  That rise athwart my path,
Why come ye here your saddening gloom
  Across my soul to cast?
Back to your haunts! I'm living now
  In light of the glad to-day;
I weep no more o'er vanished joys;
  Back ! back, ye must not stay !

Why linger ye with shadowy hands
  That point my memory back
To crumbled idols, lying low,
  O'er the weary, trodden track;
I close my eyes on your gloomy forms,
  And press on the upward way.
I'll weep no more over vanished joys;
  Back! back! Why do ye stay?

And yet, alas, with your presence, comes
  A yearning, I know not why,
To list to your plaintive, mournful tones,
  Though I pass so quickly by,
I fain would live in the peaceful calm,
  And light of the glad to-day.
I *will not* weep over vanished joys.
  Back—back—ye shall not stay!

Why should I grieve and mourn and sigh
  Over things that once have been?
I cannot better my kindest act,
  Nor lessen my greatest sin.
So back to your haunts ye goblin things,
  And there in oblivion stay,
I weep no more over vanished joys,
  I live in the glad To-day!

To-morrow.

THE trees green-leaved through which the breeze
  To-day is softly blowing,
The flowers that proudly rear their heads
  Beside the brooklet growing,
Inhale their perfume,—note their grace,
  Nor thought of sadness borrow;
Those flowers so fragrant, fresh and pure,
  May droop and die To-morrow.

Sweet child, beside thy mother's knee
  So innocent and smiling,
With childish prattle,—baby wiles,
  Her every care beguiling.
O clasp him mother while you may!
  Shield his young life from sorrow;
Thy boy, so bright and winsome now,
  Chill Death may claim To-morrow.

Young wife, close by thy husband's side,
  So beautiful and charming,
Thy pure, confiding, wifely heart
  No fear of ill alarming,
Smile while you may—love while you can,
  (God turn each poisoned arrow),
The one you trust so fondly now,
  Cold "change" may touch To-morrow.

Yea, flowers and beauty, light and joy,
  Youth, talent, love and pleasure,
The careless heart, the lovelit eye,
  Each fondly cherished treasure,
Enjoy to-day,—another sun
  May bow thy soul in sorrow,
And what you prize so dearly now,
  May all be gone To-morrow.

———

And yet new forms spring up around,
  With life the dead replacing;
The Present with its joys and cares,
  All else almost erasing,
Keep fast thy hold on Faith and Hope,
  Nor yield to needless sorrow,
The sky so dark with clouds to-day,
  May sunlit be To-morrow.

Learn to Walk Alone.

THIS world's a puzzle hard to solve,
  A riddle hard to read;
And those who find life's path *all* bright
  Are precious few indeed.
Yet don't despair though fortune frown,
  Nor murmur at your fate,
Your aim in life by earnest toil,
  You'll sure win soon or late;
But *walk upon your own feet*, friend,
  Don't trust to others strength
To carry or to pull you up
  Life's hill of weary length.
If e'er you hope to "make your mark,"
  Or let your worth be known,
Take all the props from under you
  And learn to walk alone.

Men, who depend on borrowed gold
  To brighten up your name,
And plead you *must* make such display,
  Your future wealth to gain;
Beware! "pay as you go" is best;
  Debt is an ugly foe,
You cannot tell what hour the fiend
  Will strike a fatal blow!
Sons! stand without your father's aid,
  Upon yourselves rely,
Rich fruitage in the future lies,
  You'll win it if you try.
Know that the "solid man" is he
  (In high or humble home),
Who has no props to lean upon,
  But walks along alone.

What do we Live For ?

WHAT do we live for ? Is it to toil
    And hoard up wealth we can never use ?
To labor on ever, day by day,
Till our eye and cheek their lustre lose ?
To turn our backs on life's joys and light,
And concentrate all our thoughts to gain,
Till our hair is gray and our stép grows slow,
And our body is racked with declining pain?

What do we live for? Is it that we
May rule or conquer our fellow-men?
Or is it that we may pass our time
In study of art or use of pen?
And fill the dreamless hours of night
With longings for what we cannot attain,
Or to sacrifice all our youth's bright light
For the poor and empty bauble, fame?

What do we live for? Is it to be
Despondent and saddened fore'er and e'er,
To turn from the pleasant walks of life
And choose for our part the toil and care?
Is it for this, alas, that man
Lives on, and on, through Time's long hours?
Is it for this that He has formed
Us after His image by His power?

Not so ! O tired and brain-worn hordes
In the city's heated and pent-up walls;
O drop for a while your books and pens,
Come listen how sweetly the wild bird calls!
Come gaze upon Nature's features fair,
Let her fan your brow with her perfumed breath;
Each day awhile with her scenes commune,
And life of its care will be half bereft.

A little of wealth will do us all,
If we pay our way from day to day,
And poverty is not bitter, friend,
If we have our health and a heart that's gay.
Enjoy on this earth its beauties rare,
Death rings full soon for us all his knell;
And he who has gleaned the most of joy,
Can truly say *"He has lived life well!"*

Push Ahead and Don't Despair.

DOES your path look dark and gloomy?
  Do your steps lag on the way?
 Are you weary, sad, disheartened
 At your trials every day?
 Lift your head and pass on boldly,
 Fearless, face life's storms and care;
 Every soul must bear its troubles:
 Push ahead and don't despair.

Do you toil to win an object
Far away from present view?
Does each day seem ever bringing
Added care and toil to you?
If *you do your very best*, friend,
Through all weather, foul or fair,
Sure success will crown your efforts:
Push ahead and don't despair.

What's the use to sit repining
O'er the ills we cannot mend?
Don't give way to vain repining,
Useless folly 'tis, my friend;
Don't stand moping in the shadow,
Step out where the sun shines fair,
Though the stumbling-blocks are many,
Push ahead and don't despair.

Life's Workers.

If you've incited fellow men
　To better acts and nobler deeds,—
If you have lent a friendly hand
　To help a poor man's many needs,—
If you have Charity's silence kept,
　Nor added blot to tarnished name,
But helped the weak one on his feet,—
　Be sure you have not lived in vain.

If you have shown youthful minds
　The difference 'twixt right and wrong,
Or helped to carry some one's load
　Of care Life's weary road along;
If through your means some fallen one
　Shall turn back from her life of shame
And, with God's help, live honestly,—
　Be sure you have not lived in vain.

If you shall point the way to light
　To some dark, sad, discouraged heart,
If e'er you strive to help the Right
　As in Life's scenes you take your part—
Believe our God, whose searching eye
　Knows all our motives, acts and pain,
Will not condemn His handiwork,
　Nor deem that you have lived in vain.

Your Fortune.

Shall I tell your fortune ?   Well, get the cards,
  A gypsy must have her cards, you know.
Now, sit down there with attentive mien,
  Sit right down opposite me--there--so ;
I'll shuffle and cut and con the pack,
  And all I tell will be strictly true ;
As I view the cards I will tell, my friend,
What the dim, far future will bring to you.

Your life will be checkered here and there
  With sunshine and shadow—a little rain.—
If you use your talents and aim up high,
  You'll make an honored and noble name.
. If you work and save as you go along,
  And wrong no man (by the cards I'm told),
You'll live a contented and peaceful life.
  And have wealth to spare when you grow old.

You will love (I am safe in saying that,
  For every one loves sometime in life).
If you woo her rightly you'll gain her heart,
  And make her your well beloved wife.
If you treat her e'er as a partner dear,
  And are kind and patient (the cards now say),
She'll be fond and tender and true to you,
  And be a good, faithful wife alway.

You can gain a stand in the busy world
  By earnest, faithful and ceaseless toil;
You can ride on the crest of Life's wild waves—
  Or sink unseen in the turbid moil,
The power's within you to drown or swim,
  To win wealth, laurels, friends, or lose them.
The talents you have,—how much you gain,
  Depends entire on—how you use them.

Away with this folly, your "Fortune's" done,
   I've told you all in the future lies,
As far as I can—for the coming years
   Are solemnly sealed from mortal eyes.
Your future fortune your own hands hold,
   You can mold it just as you will, I say.
Be sure, Tomorrow'll take care of itself
   If you do the best you can To-day.

My wish,

Let me be happy while I may,
To me Life's sky looks clear to-day.
Don't tell me if you know the sun
Will shroud in clouds, e'er the day is done.
Don't tell me, if the friends I love
You know, in time, most false will prove.
But let me dream and smile to-day,
Let me be happy while I may.

Perhaps the hands I love to clasp
Will smite me cruelly at last,
Perhaps the lips I love to kiss
With scorn will end my fancied bliss,
Perhaps the smiles that beam on me
Will prove to be hypocrisy,
Yet do not tell me if you know,
Don't warn me of the coming blow.

But let me dream ! Life's joys are few,
So let me fancy all are true.
Time soon for me to weep may come,
And bitter wrongs to me be done,
Yet do not cloud my dreams to-day,
These dreams that are so glad and gay,
But let me think they'll ever stay,
Let me be happy, while I may.

Rely Upon Yourself.

AS YOU go forth in busy life
   And join in the ceaseless strife,
      To gain a little wealth,
This caution I would give to you:
True hearted friends are very few,
      Trust no one but yourself.

You'll find that as a general rule,
The world will make of you a tool
      For gain of paltry pelf.
So when you form a goodly plan,
Don't tell your thought to any man,
      But " run the thing " yourself.

These so-called friends will often be
Far from you, if adversity
      E'er robs you of your wealth.
The truest friends in all the lands,
You'll find are your hard-working hands.
      Rely upon yourself.

So don't forget the motto, friend,
If you into your life would send
      True cheerfulness and health;
Remember, he's the happiest man
Who, 'mid all circumstances, can
      Rely upon himself.

Ode to Night.

O NIGHT! O quiet night!
Bathed in the clear starlight,
Bringing to weary souls
Sweet rest and calm repose;
Casting o'er grass and flowers
Bright, sparkling, dewy showers
From heaven's pure cell.

Thine is the stilly hour
When those in trouble sore,
And those who mourn their dead
With sad, low bending head
Find for their bitter grief,
Transient, but sweet relief,
In sleep's calm spell.

On thy soft winds, ascend
Prayers from the saints, who bend
Humbly at His great throne,
Whose mighty power alone,
Can to the troubled heart
Comfort and peace impart;
And heaven at last.

O night, thine is the hour,
When my mind's mighty power,
Traces on swiftest wings
All my life's wanderings;
Bringing back unto me
Plainly, the memory
Of days long past.

O night ! unto my breast
        Bring sweet forgetfulness;
   Let not my mind e'er stray
   Back o'er youth's joyous way,
Or pluck from past away,
        One brilliant, blissful day,
   Or careless hour.

O night ! unto my heart
        Sweet, quiet peace impart;
   Teach my wild, roving thought
   To deem the past as nought,
And lift my eyes above;
        Trusting in His great love
   And mighty power.

The Storm.

TO-NIGHT the storm-king holds o'er earth his sway,
  The lightning flashes—the thunder roars,
And from the lurid sky, so pitchy black,
  The rain in heavy torrents ceaseless pours.

Fair Luna hides behind the heavy clouds,
  Her beams of shining limpid, silver bright
And not a star lends to the gloomy scene
  Its ray of brilliant and mysterious light.

Anon the dazzling lightning flash reveals
  The hill, the plain, unto my watchful eyes,
Then vanishes the strange electric flash,
  Again the earth in solemn blackness lies.

Rave on, O storm! thou suitest well my mind.
  Flash! lightning, flash! and let my longing eyes
Dream that your glittering tracks are rays of light
  Shed from the opening gates of Paradise.

Dreams.

I dreamt,
　'Twas of a garden rich with lovely flowers,
　Whose gaudy hues and fragrance sweet and rare,
Filling the air, and o'er my senses stealing
　Like magic wild, beguiled my every care.

I dreamt,
'Twas of a tree whose limbs wild birds were filling;
　Their free, glad songs my sleeping soul enchanted,
Their plumage gay the while my eye delighting
　As glimpse of heaven or land by fairies haunted.

I dreamt,
'Twas of a hall; bright lights were throwing
　Their lustre o'er a board with dainties spread;
The woods, fields, sea, the vineyards,—all,
　To the rich hoard their choicest treasures sped.

I dreamt,
'Twas of a scene where wealth and pomp,
　In regal state their empty tokens flaunted;
I saw in all that lordly crowd not one
　To whom the boon of happiness was granted.

I dreamt,
'Twas of a ball-room; nimble feet were gliding
　Over the floor, to music whose sweet measure
Bewildered every sense, causing the heart to throb
　With joy delirious, lost to all but pleasure.

I dreamt,
It was of forms, whose lightest touch
　Filled me with rapture; Dream of joy!
Then flowers and song and gilded hall of pride,
　All sunk to naught in bliss without alloy.

I dreamt,
Their words were truth; ah, happy dream!
  That fled too soon,—like morning dew,
Like mist before the sun away it sped,
  Like lightning flash or sunset's glorious hue.

I dreamt,
'Twas of an eye whose glance sought mine in love,
  My spirit answering to the look
All else forsook; alas, the vision fled,
  Dreamland was gone and starting I awoke.

I 'woke and found my garlands withered leaves;
  I 'woke and found my grain was empty sheaves;
I 'woke and found my birds were birds of prey;
  I 'woke and found the music passed away.

I wept to find of truth and love no token;
  I wept to find how lightly vows are broken;
I wept to find my kind friends all had flown,
  I wept to find my bright hopes all o'erthrown.

Ah dreams of beauty, song and light,
  And friends so true; ye come no more
My soul to cheer; but through the gloom
  I onward look to heaven's bright shore.

Unrest.

MY mind to-night is not at rest,
  My spirit heaves within my breast,
    And almost seems to take its flight
    To yonder heaven so pure and bright,
      And soar beyond the stars.

My mind's keen eye can almost see
The brilliant marvelous mystery,
That holds within yon wondrous space
Each whirling planet in its place,
　　Through all Time's fleeting hours.

My spirit seems to roam at will
From planet unto planet, till
At last the moon's clear shining beams
Sink low beneath the silent streams,
　　And naught of night remains.

Then doth my spirit fold its wings
And as the morning light begins,
Worn with its toilsome wanderings,
And restless, roving hoverings,
　　Back to the earth return.

Memories.

WITH the moonbeams round me streaming,
In my chamber I sit dreaming,
　　Dreaming of bright hopes o'erthrown ;
And my spirit, sad and weary,
Clings with feeling lone and dreary
　　To the happy days long flown.

All the world is wrapped in sadness ;
Not a sound disturbs the stillness
　　Save the sighing of the wind,
Whose low and mournful sobbing
Softly calms my heart's wild throbbing,
　　Gently rests my troubled mind.

And old mem'ries round me thronging,
Fill my bosom with wild longing,
   To live childhood's bright years o'er ;
To tear out Life's written pages,
And in scorn of wise old sages,
   Be a careless child once more.

Round me visions gather thickly
Of the ones I loved so fondly,
   Of the ones so true and dear.
And though their forms I see not,
And their voices dear I hear not,
   I can feel their presence near.

Thus my spirit sadly musing,
All forgetfulness refusing,
   Lingers fondly o'er the past,
Till my heart that throbs so wildly,
And my thoughts so drear and lonely,
   Gentle slumber calms at last.

The Sea,

YOU may sing of the beauties of flowers and trees,
   Of the fresh, green woodland's mysteries,
Of halls that resound with wit and mirth,
Of wonders hidden deep in the earth ;
You may sing their praises, but ah ! to me
There is nothing so dear as the rolling sea.

How wildly and madly the white waves play,
How they fling and splash their brilliant spray;
They come rushing in with a roaring tone,
And then glide back with a sob, and moan;
Nought of nature is half as dear to me
As thou, O, tossing, restless sea.

I love to sit on thy glittering sand,
Or wander alone on thy sunny strand,
And gather the pebbles and quaint, queer shells,
Cast up from thy hidden, unknown cells.
O, would I knew all thy mystery,
O moaning, sobbing, sighing sea !

O sea, as thy waves so memories come
To me, of the days when gay and young,
I mingled (O happy time to me),
'Mong those now severed far from me.
Some in strange countries took their way,
And others have gone to a brighter day.

Roll on, O sea ! for far away
Is my roving mind and heart to-day.
Perhaps thy music can drive from me
The grief for those I no more will see.
So cheer my soul with thy sturdy roar,
And I will think of the past no more.

The Coat makes the man of today.

THERE'S many queer sayings we hear every day,
    And some are quite " stale," some are new;
But the one I will mention in this little rhyme
Is something, alas, that's " too true."
No matter how gifted or worthy you be,
As you hurry along on life's way,
If seedy your clothes, you'll be slighted andscorned;
For the coat makes the man of to-day.

A man may be vile as the vilest can be;
If he cloaks all his sin beneath gold,
Now-a-days he is sought after, fawned on and praised,
And looked up to by both young and old.
While he legally plunders his poor fellow-men,
Grinds the hearts of the poor day by day;
His wealth shuts the eyes of his friends to his crimes,
For the coat makes the man ofto-day

Degenerate mankind, alas, cherish gold
And fine clothes, more than virtue and brains;
And the man who can spend out the most for display,
The highest position attains.
But the day will soon come when a man's honest worth
Will stamp him—and people will say:
"Give us honor and truth, and not tinsel and dross,"
Though the coat makes the man of to-day.

The Four Suns.

HE was a laughing, bright-eyed merry boy,
Who romped and played with heart so light and gay,
With his young mates, while o'er the distant hills
Shone warm the fading light of summer's day.
Tne sunset tinted all the scene with gold,
Yet all unheeded passed the glad hours by,
Till at the homestead door his mother stands,
And gazes on the scene with lovelit eye,
And soon I hear her say, "Come home, my pet,
'T is time my little boy was safe in bed—
     The sun has set."

The years roll by ; the boy to manhood grown,
With bearded cheek and form erect and strong,
Has singled out from loveliest womankind
The one to cherish most through all life long.
Implicit faith he places in her truth,
Affection gives the holiest man can pay,
Alas ! as time flies by he finds her false,
His joy-crowned future passes slow away ;
Heart-broken though he be, he knows not yet
That from his life the brightest light has gone—
                Love's sun has set.

Years still glide on among life's busiest throng.
We find him now—Ambition rules his soul ;
He strives 'gainst poverty, hate, malice—all—
Works with a will to win the wished-for goal.
Alas ! his step grows slow, his eyes grow dim,
His idle hands hang listless by his side ;
Into vice, drunkenness and shame
He careless drifts upon life's changing tide ;
His guardian angel's eyes with tears are wet,
His warning voice is all unheeded now—
                Hope's sun has set.

A few more years, and then an humble hearse
Passes along the dusty, worn highway,
Bearing away to rest and peace at last
The poor, world-worn, spirit-broken clay.
No funeral knell rings out upon the air,
No mourners gather round the humble tomb ;
His friends, the few he had, are scattered far,
Or else are careless what may be his doom.
But in the great Hereafter he may yet
Find what he vainly sought on earth—
                Life's sun has set.

Philosophy.

SOMETIMES the cross we have to bear
  Seems far too heavy for our strength,
And often do our footsteps lag
  Along life's path of weary length.
Yet push ahead, the way *will* clear,
  These stumbling blocks *must* be withstood;
And oft events that seem the worst
  Are very often for our good.

Do friends betray the love you gave,
  And prove themselves of little worth ?
Don't let that cloud your happiness,
  Nor banish from your heart the mirth.
Your love was pure—*your* truth unstained,
  To *them*, not you, falls all the shame.
You've learned a lesson, that is all;
  You know " the burnt child dreads the flame."

Live in yourself, 'tis better far;
  For " friends " so often fail us now;
Then stand alone and meet your fate
  With steady heart and fearless brow.
Press on your way, the road *will* clear,
  The storms of life must be withstood;
You'll find events that seem the worst
  Are very often for our good.

Passing thoughts.

ON SEEING A HANDSOME BOUQUET.

O FLOWERS, sweet flowers,
  So fragrant and so fair,
Whose perfume sweet is wafted on the air;
    You charm my senses
    And delight my eye;
      Why must you die ?

Bright, laughing child,
Whose dancing, fairy feet
 Trip by me now so merrily and neat;
You, in whose heart
Is happiness untold,
 Must you grow old ?

O, maiden fair,
Of beauty's fairest mould,
 Whose charms I view, so choice and manifold,
'Tis sad to think,
Bewitching, lovely maid,
 Your charms will fade !

Sweet thoughts
God planted in our minds;
 Whose presence lightens up our cross in life;
 Remembrance of our loved, that like a sun,
 Shines on our hearts through all the world's
Ye, while life lasts,   [mad strife;
And reason holds its sway,
 Pass not away.

The Old Dress,

WELL, yes, it is " shabby," don't laugh at it, pray,
Just fold it up neatly and put it away.
Poor, worn-out dress! I will keep it fore'er,
As I would a choice picture or lock of friend's hair.
I will keep it and prize it through all life's strange changes,
The dress that I wore when I earned my first wages.

Poor " green " little girl ! I can smile now, you see,
As the place and the scene in thought come to me,
As with loud-beating heart I stood waiting my " cue,"
And trembled lest failure attend my " debut."
Though greater acts now my attention engages,
I prize the old dress that helped earn my first wages.

What labor it cost me you'll sure understand,
When I say every part was made by my own hand.
How I worried for fear the few charms I possessed
Should not on that night appear at their best.
Time flies.   Since that night I have trod many stages,
Yet I keep the old dress that helped earn my first wages.

Poor faded old dress ! there all crumpled you lie,
Your days of " utility " all have passed by.
You seem an old friend !· " I am foolish," you say.
Perhaps so ; yet carefully put it away.
'Tis " useless," I know, but through life's busy changes,
I'll keep the old dress that helped earn my first wages.

HUMOROUS.

" Old Yaller,"

-OR " BETTING MONEY ON THE WRONG DOG."

THIS happened way out in the " diggins,"
   An' Bill run a gin-shop out thar;
He was sort of an onery customer,
   With a squint an' a shock o' red hair.
He had an old dog he called " Yaller,"
   Bill said he was great on the fight;
But Lord! we thought he was lyin,'
   Or talkin' because he was tight.

But it seems Bill, over in England,
   Was a "dog fightin' man," as they say,
An' that this here mean-lookin' old " Yaller,"
   Had licked every dog in his way.
He was a meek lookin' old cretur',
   He'd "make-up" with the men old an' young,
But a rale rip-tarer when started,
   As you'll see when my story is done.

One day a young chap struck the "diggins,"
   He was travelin' on to New York
With a bull-purp—could lick a hyena—
   To believe all *his* long-winded talk.

Durn my skin, but his dog was a stunner,
  Trim an' stout, iron-jawed an' red-eyed;
An' none on us doubted the cretur
  Could show rale game fight when he tried.

Wal, this chap an' his dog was one mornin'
  Sort o' loafin' around nigh Bill's bar,
When old "Yaller" came trottin' in meek-like,
  (He allus was sneakin' round thar);
The bull purp started for "Yaller,"
  But the New York chap collared his pup,
And hollered out, "Shut up that dorg thar,
  If you don't want him total chawed up."

"You see this dorg's trained for a fighter,
  An' when he sees dorg, black or white,
He'll pitch in, if I ain't a watchin',
  An' chaw the same dorg out of sight.
I'd hate like the devil to have him
  Kill that good-natured old dorg o' yourn,
But keep him tied up while I'm here, Bill,
  Or he's gone dorg sure as you're born."

Bill grinned, then he said, "why, old 'Yaller,'
  He's no good—all the time in the way,
'Spose we have a dorg-fight in the bar-room,
  Come stranger, what do you say,
An' to make the thing sort o' excitin'
  As 'Yaller's' my dorg, I'll just bet
One hundred, he, in ten minutes,
  Will clean out yer prize-fightin' pet."

"Poor 'Yaller,'" says Bill, sort o' soft-like,
  "Yer time has most come for to die,"
An' "Yaller" looked up—tail a waggin',
  With a kind o' sly wink in his eye;

An' Bill hollered out, " come on in boys,
    Come an' see this 'ere prize-fightin' pup,
(We must have some little excitement),
    So, he's goin' to chaw ' Yaller ' up."

Wal we come in, each man held his dorg thar;
    Old " Yaller " was snarlin' like mad,
An' you bet the bull-purp was a snappin'
    A lookin' most all-fired bad.
At the word the dorgs met—in a minnit
    " Yaller " had the prize dorg by the throat,
An' he shook, an' he chawed, never givin'
    The bull-purp a chance for a holt.

An' he shook till the purp " kicked the bucket,"
    Then he trotted quite cool like away
As if he'd done nothin' uncommon,
    But chawed up bull-purps every day;
An' Bill gobbled up the bet money,
    Smilin' like at the defunct bull-purp,
An' says he, *"Who else here's got a dorg now*
    That wants to chaw old 'Yaller' up?"

The city chap sneaked off quite quiet,
    An' left for New York the next day;
Old " Yaller " is trottin' around yet,
    Quite innercent-like in his way;
Bill's jolly as ever—an' boastin'
    An' braggin' about his old purp,
An' never gets tired a tellin',
    How the prize dorg chawed old " Yaller " up.

"I Want my Balloon."

A S I walked down the street one bright sunny day,
 A comical sight met my gaze;
A scene that for mixture of sorrow and fun,
 Will haunt me through all of my days.
On the walk stood a child, who with "Injun-like" yells
 Of dismay, stared up to the sky,
Where a tiny, red object was floating away
 And fast growing dim to the eye.
As nearer I came he loudly bawled out,
 "I don't want to lose it so soon,
O please catch it quickly! O make it come back!
 I want my nice, pretty balloon!"

"Little lad," then I said, "it will never return;
 Why did you let go of the string?
Pray did you not know when you loosened your hold,
 Your plaything would surely take wing?"
"Why ma'am," sobbed the child, "I thought it would stay
 And float close above me, until
I wearied of watching it bob up and down,
 And could draw it back to me at will.
O, won't you please stop it? it's floating away!
 I don't want to lose it so soon!
O somebody catch it! it's going so fast!
 Do stop my nice, rosy balloon!"

Ah! many there be in this world's busy throng
 Who held in *their* hands the frail string
That bound to themselves wealth, laurels or love,
 Or some other valuable thing.
But alas! like the child, they loosened their grasp,
 Perhaps merely testing their power,

But realized too late what their recklessness wrought,
   As they watched it soar 'bove them so far;
Then frantic they strove their hold to regain,
   But too oft 'tis humanity's doom,
To, by their own folly, lose what they prize most,
   And then cry for their vanished balloon!

My Choice.

BY A GIRL OF THE PERIOD.

I'D HAVE a lover brave and true,
   A fond adorer ever;
Who'll woo me with untiring zeal,
   And be inconstant never;
Who'll boldly seek and gain u y hand,
   And "bounce" each other "feller,"
Who if a rival dared approach,
Would hit him on the "smeller."

I'd have him have a heart and soul
   O'erflowed with truth and daring,
Who knew his rights and claimed them too,
   Without a shade of fearing;
Who'd ever press his earnest suit
   With honest, manly spirit;
Who'd want my love, and dare to strive
   Before all men to win it.

Some girls would like a handsome chap,
   Who brings them rings and candy;
Some like a man with lots of "tin,"
   And some could love a dandy.

Some like a timid chap who e'er
  'Twixt hope and fear doth hover,
But none of these could suit *my* mind,
  I want a dashing lover.

He need not be so very rich,
  If he do love but me,
And does not flirt with other girls
  When I'm not near to see;
If such a fellow breathes on earth
  On him my heart is set,
And when I catch a sight of him
  I'll "set my cap" you bet.

Wanted: A wife.

BY A BACHELOR.

I'M WHAT the cold world calls a "bach,"
  I'm looking for a wife,
Some gentle and obedient girl,
  To bless my lonely life;
I've waited now for forty years
  But never met my doom,
And so to-day I advertise,
  In hopes to find her soon.

I have a span of splendid grays,
  A "nobby" carriage too,
Have lots of "stamps,"—am 5 ft. 6—
  Kind, generous and true.
But, to all widows seeing this,
  I herewith do imply,
That I abhor all "relics," so
  No widows need apply!

And to old maids both tall and short,
　I solemnly do state,
That I would sooner die, than have
　A spinster for my mate;
Their fate waits toward the setting sun,
　They'll please the men there best,
To spinsters, I (like Greeley) say,
　"Go west," old girls, "go west."

I want a lovely, sprightly miss
　Of eighteen years, or *less*,
With raven hair and eyes of jet,
　And greatest taste in dress;
She must be learned and rich—to such
　A willing slave am I,
And here I say to one and all,
　No others need apply.

"Toot yer Horn if you don't sell a Clam

WHILE on a trip to Baltimore,
　That city grand on Chesapeake's shore,
I met a man upon the pier,
　('Mong other venders standing near;)
With clams his cart was loaded down,
　(A peddler he about the town.)
"Good man," said I, "how many hours
Will it take to sell that load of yours?"
He turned and said, "Well I don't know,
Whether I'll sell 'em fast or slow,
Life is a sort of game of 'grab,'
An' nothin' venture, nothin' have,
I'll do *my* best as sure as you're born,
I'll go around an' toot my horn
If I don't sell a clam!"

He drove away; his horn's clear(?) swell
Told far and near he'd clams to sell;
"Toot! toot! clams! c-l-a-m-s!" I heard him call,
"Here's nice fresh clams for great and small."
"Toot! clams!" he called from street to street,
To all whom he would chance to meet.
I watched him drive out of my sight,
Yet still I heard his voice of might
Yell "clams! clams! clams!" I smiled to see
The honest fellow's earnest zeal.
I sauntered on with careless tread,
And still those words rang in my head,
"I'll do *my* best as sure as you're born,
I'm goin' 'round to toot my horn
If I don't sell a clam!"

I learned a lesson from that man,
I honored his hard-working plan,
I pray you take it home likewise.
Despondent souls with heavy eyes
"Brace up," that's slang I know, but true,
And good advice for me and you.
Don't sit and loaf on life's curbstone,
While others pass you're left alone.
"Git up and git," don't waste your time,
Life's choicest prizes may be thine;
Good luck awaits both rich and poor,
Go round and hunt—you'll find it sure.
Don't sit complaining so forlorn,
Go rush around and "toot your horn"
If you don't sell a clam.

"I'll Bet Yer a Dollar,"

'TIS strange how betting is "coming in style,"
     All bet, both the great and the small,
And precious few people we meet now-a-days
     Who do no betting at all.
"I'll bet you a dollar" 's the favorite sum now,
     So I'll "fall in" and "follow in line,"
And bet with the rest as my pen scribbles off
     This simple and rough little rhyme.

If you meet a man who is "seedy" and poor,
     And not got a cent to his name,
If you reach out your hand and help him along,
     Once more independence to gain,
When he gets a firm stand by your liberal aid,
     And is well up Prosperity's hill,
He may vow that your kindness he'll never forget,
     But, "I bet yer a dollar" he will.

A young gentleman escorts a young lady home
     From a party or ball as may be,
And stops at the gate for a moment or so,
     And longs for a kiss,—do you see?
If he snatch one the lady may hurry away
     With the look of a much injured saint,
And vow " she's insulted " and " terribly vexed! "
     But " I bet yer a dollar " she ain't.

An old bachelor sits in his dingy old room,
     With a scowl on his crabbed old face;
With no children to prattle around his hearth-stone,
     ·And no kind wife his table to grace,
He may sneer at young couples, and call them "poor fools,"
     Laugh to scorn each proud, happy young " dad;"
He may swear he is pleased with his bachelor state,
     But "I'll bet yer a dollar" he's sad.

But I'll close now my silly and strange little verse,
  And afflict the kind reader no more,
If indeed anybody has patience enough
  To con these rude sentences o'er;
Don't find fault, I pray, nor ask "where's the sense
  Of this rambling poem(?) or rant ;"
Don't insist that the meaning to you I make plain,
  For "I bet yer a dollar" I can't.

Deacon Gray.

OLD Deacon Gray was as mean a man
  As I've seen for many a day;
He'd steal and lie for the sake of a dime,
And rob all who came in his way.
He'd steal the cents from a dead man's eyes,
Yet loud would he cant and pray.
"So much ahead," he'd say to himself
As he hoarded the pennies away.

Yet Deacon Gray was a " pious " man,
He was member of church and choir,
Though he starved his children and wife—and beat
His poor laborers out of their hire.
He stole a cow from his neighbor's herd—
Stole wood from his neighbor's pile.
"So much ahead," said Deacon Gray,
" I'll be rich in a little while!"

Well, Deacon Gray he died one day,
Like the rest of poor human race,
And his soul went out of its case of clay,
And soared to unknown space.
The Devil met him with leer and grin,
For the Devil's heart was gay,
" I'm a soul ahead. Come on, ha ! ha ! "
Said the Devil to Deacon Gray.

"Big Injun."

HE came and sat by our camp fire
　With a savage's proud disdain.
He was gaudy with paint and feathers,
"Big Eagle" was his name.
I asked him to tell of his exploits,
Of deeds that gained him his fame,
And he folded his blanket about him,
And began in the following strain:

"Me Uncle Sam's good Injun,
Me big chief of Cheyenne ;
Me steal—me cuss—drink firewater,
All same like pale face men ;
Me got me squaws heap plenty,
Pappooses me got nine;
Heap much good grub and blankets,
Have heap much bully good time ;
Nine moons me go on war-path,
Kill much—steal ponies heap;
By by Injun tired out fighting,
Uncle Sam send coffee—bread—meat—
Then Injun go back to wigwam—
Much cold—ground all over snow.
When summer-time come, then me fight more;
Then me go to Washington*—maybe so
Uncle Sam forget 'bout Injun,
No send 'nough coffee—bread—meat,
Then Injun him kill *a-ll* soldiers,
Burn ranch—scalp—steal—much heap.
Now all time me good Injun ;
Big Eagle great chief—no lie—
Me got good grub and blankets—
Uncle Sam—bully boy—glass eye."

* It s the ardent wish of most of the chiefs of the different reservations to be
. sent on to Washington.

O ravers o'er pitiful stories
Of the " poor persecuted red men,''
If you want to be cured of your folly,
Come and gaze on the noble (?) Cheyenne.

A Woman's Explanation,

WELL, yes, I did go walking
   On yesterday with Jim,
But, Jack, you know, he's but a friend,
   You needn't care for him.
We walked down in the woodland,
   The bird's sweet songs to hear.
He squeezed my hand—but—but—I fancied
   He was *you*, my dear.

Last week we went out sailing,
   A few miles down the bay;
I went to help pass time, dear Jack,
   While you were far away.
His arm got round my waist,
   But *how*, I never can make clear;
He—kissed me once—but—but—I *fancied*
   He was you, my dear.

There now ! he's gone ! and angry too !
   What have I said that's wrong?
He thinks when he's away, I should
   Sit grieving all day long !
" I flirt ?" " I false ! "   Well, I declare,
   I'll spoil his little plan !
Ill never speak to him again,
   The wretched, jealous man.

HOME POEMS.

Somebody's Waiting for me,

WHEN the sunlight slowly fading,
　　Proclaims the dying day,
And across the fields and meadows
　　I homeward take my way,
Just down the turn in the pathway
　　'Neath the shade of that old oak tree,
There's somebody, mild and gentle,
　　Who watches and waits for me.

She stands in the waning sunshine,
　　With the lovelight in her eye,
And her wind-swung tresses floating
　　O'er a cheek of crimson dye.
With a smile of joyous welcome
　　To meet me she gaily trips,
And a tender kiss awaits me
　　From somebody's loving lips.

I name not her age or station,
　　If humble or proud she be,
But of all the heaven-given treasures
　　The dearest and best is she.

Too kind for a thought of evil,
    E'er willing my cares to share,
The queen of my heart's deep centre
    Is she who is waiting there.

So whatever of ill befall me,
    Through the weary and tedious day,
As the evening shadows lengthen,
    And I homeward take my way,
My heart and my step grow lighter
    As I near that old oak tree,
For I know that my darling's watching
    And waiting to welcome me.

The Old Wife's Song.

WE'RE a jolly old couple, our hair is gray,
    But never a mite care we.
Our lifeboat drifts on Time's tranquil tide,
    And from trouble and care we're free.
Our steps are slow and our frames are bent,
    There's a mist o'er our dim old eyes,
Yet cheerful we travel, hand in hand,
    'Neath pleasant or stormy skies.
Many long years we've journeyed on,
    And the end we can almost see ;
But we're ready to go when the Master calls,
    My dear old man and me.

Seventy years we struggled on,
    Our trials were not a few.
We raised our family best we could
    Till each boy into manhood grew;

Then they turned away from the threshold worn,
 Afar through the world to roam,
Till the last loved one had passed away
 From the silent and lonesome home.
Three wedded the mates that their young hearts chose;
 Two travel the restless sea;
So we live in the old house all alone,
 My dear old man and me.

We chat o'er the scenes of our youthful days,
 And we laugh right merrily
As we sit in the evening's quiet glow,
 O'er our cups of fragrant tea.
For love dies not like the soft, dark trees,
 Or the color of cheek's bright glow;
And our hearts are just as warm to-day
 As they were long years ago.
Together we stand on the mystic shore
 Of eternity's solemn sea,
And we trust we will safely cross to Him,
 My dear old man and me.

Going Home,

GOING home ! How strange it sounds to me!
I who for years have roamed o'er land and sea,
So long have clasped no hands save stranger's hands,
So long made transient "homes" in foreign lands
 I scarce can realize all the word implies.

Going home ! for rest and peace, I say,
Back to the place where first I saw the day.
Shall I indeed my old friends' faces see?
Will they indeed in true faith welcome me?
 Or shall I find, alas ! affection dies?

Going home ! I wonder if the flowers
Are still as fragrant as in childhood's hours.
I wonder if the old tree's standing yet,
Beneath whose shade I've watched the grand sunset
　Gilding the rolling prairies of the west.

Going home ! I eagerly return
Back to the hearth where dearest home-fires burn.
Though friends forget or fail to recognize,
Upon the scene I'll gaze with loving eyes,
　My home—the spot on earth I love the best.

Illinois.

I CAN hear the bells a-chiming,
　Bells that ring so loud and gay,
Yet my thoughts to-day turn backward
　To my home so far away.
Round me flowers bud and blossom,
　Softest Southern breezes blow ;
Though 't is Christmas' joyous morning,
　Yet I see no frost or snow.
I can hear the Spanish lady
　Chant her strange, yet lovely tune;
Near my window are magnolias,
　And the orange's perfume,
Yet my northern heart is restless—
　Longings wild my soul annoy,
And I'd rather see the snow gleam
　On the plains of Illinois.

I have crossed the grand old " Rockies,"
　With their snow-capped heads so high,
Gazed down in their rugged bosoms,
　Where the miners' treasures lie ;

Roamed o'er Kansas—Colorado,
    (Beauteous " Switzerland of the West,)"
Watched the turbid Rio Grande
    Rushing on in wild unrest ;
Crossed the Gila—Brazos—Pecos—
    Gleaming rivers pure and bright ;
Watched the Indians as they gathered
    Round their camp-fire's cheerful light ;
Plucked the loveliest southern blossoms,
    Perfumed sweet, without alloy,
Yet I'd rather have a violet
    From the plains of Illinois.

Wonder not my heart turns backward
    From these bright but stranger scenes;
That I'm longing for the prairies,
    With their placid, gliding streams ;
That I choose from out her sisters
    Illinois to love the best,
And that none like her can ever
    Hold first place within my breast.
Mountains, valleys, caves and canyon,
    Perfumed air, bewildering song,
Though they win me for a moment,
    Do not claim my homage long.
I will tell you now the secret
    Why I thus these scenes disown—
As a child I roamed the prairies,
    And Chicago is my home.

Love Commands All.

THERE came to a laughing country maid,
    One beautiful summer's day,
A fairy who bent at her tiny feet,
    And in accents sweet did say:
"Thy merits so please our fairy queen,
    She has now commissioned me
To give thee the choice of four noble gifts,
    Which I now will name to thee.
Thus spake my queen: ' Doth she wish for gold,
    Or honor, or love, or fame,
Say I will send her of these four things
    Whichever she choose to name.'
But ponder well ere thou choose, dear maid,
    For whatever your choice shall be,
You must cling to it through all of life
    And lose the other three."

The maiden paused and a troubled shade
    Came over her features fair;
" 'Twould be fine," she mused, "to have the gold
    With those I love to share;
But wealth alone could ne'er supply
    The wants of this heart of mine,
I can not—dare not lay my all
    At Mammon's gorgeous shrine ;
And fame and honor by such as I
    Are held but in light esteem;
We value more the woods—the flowers,
    And the sun's warm shining beam;
The pets of the world's loud praising crowds
    Oft carry a heavy heart,
And for peace of mind and health and joy
    With laurels would gladly part."

"And love—" her cheek flushed a deeper hue,
 And a soft light in her eye
Shone forth with a brilliant joyous flash,
 That rivaled the sunlit sky.
"I have pondered well o'er my choice, dear Fay,
 And I'll take of thy queen's gifts free,
The one I deem will in future years
 Prove the dearest and best to me.
I choose that I ever may be beloved
 By those whom my heart holds dear,
And that Love and I may never part,
 Through all of my journey here."
Quoth the fairy, "Thy choice is the richest one
 That is e'er to mortals given,
For a loving heart that's beloved again,
 Finds the earth almost a heaven!"

Then the light-winged fairy sped away
 To her home in the shady glade,
And told her queen of the treasure chose
 By the heart of the lovely maid.
Quoth the queen: "'Tis well with the guileless girl,
 Ho! Fairies! I charge thee, flee!
And carry to her not love alone,
 But also the other three!"

Nobody Cares but Mother.

FULL many changes old Time has wrought
   In my life, so strange—eventful ;
And few I find who cheer me on,
   But many I find who censure.
And where'er I go, and whene'er the clouds
   O'er my troubled pathway hover,
I find it still, as in childhood's hours,
   That nobody cares but mother.

If the thorns pierce deep my way-worn feet,
   And no resting-place to cheer me
Doth greet my eye, and my voice falls dead
   On ears that refuse to hear me,
How quickly my strength doth seem renewed,
   And light all my path doth cover ;
Ah ! how speedy the cross that I bear grows light
   By a cheering word from mother.

Yes, friends of to-day may be kind and true,
   And love me pure—sincerely;
But no love on earth can e'er replace
   This which I prize so dearly.
And when my journeyings all are o'er,
   My sole wish is no other
Than that kindly Fate will take me back
   To my childhood's home and mother.

Betrayed.

HE was of proud and high descent,
 She was a peasant maid.
She loved too well, alas ! alas !
 A heavy price she paid.
O sob ye winds, with solemn tone;
 Sun, hide thy face from sight,
For she, so beautiful and fair,
 Is dying with thy light!

O, bright and sparkling was her eye,
 With lips of rosy red,
A face as fresh as yonder flower,
 And raven-curl crowned head !
So wan, so feeble lies she now;
 Birds ! hush thy warblings gay;
Her lovely eyes will close for e'er
 Before another day !

A sad-eyed mother watches o'er
 Her daughter's fading life;
She is her first-born still,
 Although a mother, but no wife.
She loved—she trusted—was deceived—
 On her life fell the blight;
Aye, whisper low, ye sobbing winds,
 For she will die to-night.

 . . . .

Clasp her hands o'er her bosom calm;
 Brush smooth her silken hair ;
Place her dead baby on her breast,
 And kiss her brow so fair.
God knoweth all—He knoweth all
 The wiles her love that won.
At peace at last ! poor hapless girl !
 Thy earthly cares are done.

To My Old Friends,

O TRUE old friends ! O kind old friends,
   Dear friends I loved of yore,
Your memory dwells within my heart,
   As I roam from shore to shore.
I've traveled far 'mid splendid scenes,
   O'er mountain, hill and dell,
And many hands I've clasped in mine
   That knew and loved me well.
But new found friends supplant you not,
   Ah ! still where e'er I roam,
My heart holds fast the mem'ry of
   Dear friends who are at home.

Come clasp my hands, ye honest friends,
   That knew me from a child;
With whom so often merrily
   I weary time beguiled.
I love to feel the fervent press
   Of your dear hands again,
I long to hear your voices loved
   Call once again my name.
Time brings great changes to all lives,
   But, 'till my days are o'er,
My heart will hold a tender spot
   For my dear old friends of yore.

If.

IF I could only dream again
  The glad, bright dreams of long ago,
And tear from mem'ry's full writ page
  The scenes and deeds I so well know;
If I could only feel again
  That honest trust in human kind,
And drive the doubt and weary pain
  From out my tired, world-worn mind;

If this could be methinks whate'er
  Unto my lot might then be sent,
I'd bear with uncomplaining heart,
  And 'mid all trials be content.
Friends of my youth ! return, return !
  Kind friends of yore ! come clasp my hand
O leave me not alone to toil
  O'er life's wild, rugged land !

Vain is my call.   Their faces loved
  The scenes of earth no longer know;
Deep with my youthful dreams they're hid
  Within the grave of long ago.
I hurry on.   Few, few I meet
  Can to my heart give answering tone,
And when 'mid gay and careless crowds
  'Tis then I am the most alone.

Lines,

TO A FRIEND.

O THINK of me,
  Though now our barks upon life's troubled sea
Shall drift apart. Though it may chance to be
That never more as in the pleasant past
Our paths shall side by side again be cast.
Yet, whatsoe'er may be thy future lot,
           Forget me not.

  Remember me,
And if thou findest that the new found friends
Prove like a reed in every wind that bends,
O then bethink thee of the one afar,
Whose love shines o'er thee like a watching star,
Whose fondest thoughts are centered all on thee,
          Where'er thou be.

  But, dearest one,
If thou art beset by life's relentless storms,
If friends prove false; if thy lone spirit mourns,
And footsore, heartsick you would fain find rest
Upon a loving and a faithful breast;
If e'er (which God forbid) such time should be
          Haste unto me.

Lines,

ON HEARING A GENTLEMAN SAY THE SPIRIT OF HIS DEAD WIFE SEEMED
ALWAYS NEAR HIM.

SHE is not dead.
  I feel, I know that she is ever near,
  Her loving tones still ring upon my ear,
  And cheer my soul as in the days of yore,
  And though on earth I ne'er shall see her more,
        She has not fled.

  Her soul lives still.
It lingers ever round my onward way,
With its pure presence blessing every day.
Beloved wife ! her faith and constancy,
And her deep love, and confidence in me
        Death could not kill.

  Her graceful frame,
Whose presence filled with joy my happy home,
Is hid from view, and I am left alone.
But still her gentle spirit comes to me,
And thus, despite the grave's dark mystery,
        She lives again.

  So on in life
I journey with a cheerful, thankful heart,
And humbly bear of toil and care my part.
Soon will I clasp her cherished form once more,
Soon will I meet upon yon blissful shore
        My angel wife.

God's Christmas Gift.

'TWAS Christmas day,
　The pure snow lay
Deep over the slumbering, silent earth;
　While all around
　Was heard the sound
Of innocent, careless, heartfelt mirth.

　By rushed a throng,
　With laugh and song,
Of schoolgirls chatting of Christmas cheer;
　Unheeding one
　Who, pale and young,
And empty handed, lingered near.

　As they passed away,
　With hearts so gay,
I turned to the maiden standing near,
　And gaily said,
　As she raised her head,
" Well, what did Santa bring you, dear? "

　Her dark brown eyes
　Looked their surprise,
As she said, " O Miss, we are but poor;
　We deem it wealth,
　If perfect health
And food are plenty within our door.

　" So, Miss, you see
　That such as we
Are well content these toys to spare.
　I covet not
　A richer lot,
Of greater treasures I have a share.

"For one above
In gracious love,
This day to me has kindly given
A pleasure rare,
A gem most fair,
It is the Christian's hope of Heaven.

"Last night so plain
This message came,
'For *thee* was Jesus crucified.
He reigns above,
O. trust his love,
And He will be thy refuge—guide."

Her eyes were raised
To meet my gaze,
As she said (I still her image see),
"He died for *me*,
Low as I be,
Christ was God's Christmas gift to me."

I bowed my head,
No word I said,
A lesson deep in my heart was laid.
O would that I
Could look on high,
With the trust and faith of that little maid!

To a Child.

BRIGHT, happy childish face,
That beams with fairy grace,
  Loved one so dear;
Thy little dancing form,
Resplent with baby charm,
  Sheds sunshine here.

That little rosy palm,
And snowy, dimpled arm,
  And brow so fair,
Seems formed to bless the earth,
And change to happiness
  The darkest care.

Thy voice so sweet and clear,
And tiny feet e'er near,
  And loving heart;
Unto my troubled breast,
So full of wild unrest,
  Sweet calm impart.

Dear child in thee I find
One who with constant mind,
  Loves me alone;
Whose lisped words are truth,
Whose thoughts of honest youth
  Are all my own.

Bridal and Funeral Flowers.

"BRIDAL and funeral flowers."
  Those were the words it bore,
Shining in letters bright,
  Over the florist's door.

" Bridal and funeral flowers,"
  Coupling thus as one
The bride and the cold, stiff corse,
  Whose race of life is run.

One who will soon go forth
  A happy trusting wife,
And one who in Death's calm sleep
  Is safe from the cares of life.

As I read the words I think
  'Tis in white they robe the bride,
When she stands in modest grace
  By her chosen husband's side.

And in white they clothe the corse,
  While the cold, pale hand, perchance,
Hold the mate to the bridal flower,
  Perhaps from the self same branch.

" Bridal and funeral flowers,"
  Blooming there side by side,
To be placed in the dead's cold hand,
  Or twined in the hair of the bride.

"Bridal and funeral flowers."
  Happiness—death and gloom,
Written thus side by side,
  Life—and the dark, cold tomb.

But who is the one to tell
　　Which is most truly blest?
The bride in her youthful pride,
　　Or the one who is safe at rest?

Under the Willow,

UNDER the willow I stand to-night,
　And the stars above shed solemn light
O'er the scene I have come to view once more,
Ere I leave forever my native shore.

Under the willow I stand and gaze
On the ruined home of my youthful days;
What vanished bliss my heart recalls,
　As I look on the stained and crumbled walls.

Within that home I was born and bred ;
There sounded my sisters' and brothers' tread.
In that home was spent the happy years
Ere I faced the world with its toil and fears.

Within its walls died, one by one,
The loving parents, the children young ;
And I alone, am left to gaze
On its ruined walls, 'neath the stars calm rays.

Can all these years have passed ?　It seems
But a day, when amid these remembered scenes ;
Though my eye then bright, is dimmed now,
And deep, dark wrinkles mark my brow.

Home, churchyard willow ! I leave you all ;
Those long past years I cannot recall ;
The pain it costs me I cannot tell,
To turn away with a sad farewell.

Lines

ON THE DEATH OF A CHILD.

DEARLY loved one, thou hast vanished,
   Thy bright baby form has perished;
     Thou art now beyond the stars.
Never more we'll hear thee singing,
With thy voice so clear and ringing ;
     Mem'ry only now is ours.

Though my heart is full of sadness,
And my life seems void of gladness,
     Since thy childish form has fled ;
Still, I would not now recall thee ;
Better far that thou should'st calmly
     Slumber with the quiet dead.

Better, e'er thy heart so blithesome,
Learned how sad, and drear and toilsome
     Is the lot of all on earth ;
E'er the time when thou would'st sadly
Wish thy mother, (grieving fondly,)
     Ne'er had given thee thy birth.

'Round thy grave bright flowers are springing,
And the notes of wild birds singing,
     Fill the air at eventide.
O'er thy headstone, coldly gleaming,
Summer sun so brightly streaming,
     Seemeth longest to abide.

Peaceful is thy quiet slumber ;
Thou among the heavenly number,
     Safe from care will ever be.
When my journey is completed,
May we then be re-united
     In the glad Eternity.

My bird's song.

'TIS a stormy day and the heavy clouds
    Hang low, with a frowning mein ;
The rain pours down, and no friendly ray
    From old hidden Sol is seen.
I sit alone in my study here,
    And wish that the clouds were gone,
While Dick, my bird, in his cage near by
    Sings to me through the storm.

Anon the clouds of the deepest dye
    Are cleft by the lightning's flash,
And the rain with fury fierce and wild,
    'Gainst my window pane doth dash.
But Dick unheeds the dark outside ;
    (In the South first he saw the dawn),
And as if he was 'mong his native hills,
    Sings to me through the storm.

And I smile as I hear his merry lay,
    As it rings so quaint and sweet,
As I watch the poise of his dainty head,
    And the dance of his busy feet.
My eye grows bright, and my weary brain
    Forgets it is racked and worn,
And I say " sing on, my merry bird,
    O sing to me through the storm."

O, would that all in this selfish world,
    In the hurrying, grasping throng,
Could have in their souls a hidden hope,
    Or a love that is deep and strong,
That would light their lives with a gleam of light
    When time leaves them bereft and worn,
And ring in their hearts through the world's mad strife
    Like my bird's song through the storm.

Footsteps on the Stair,

SITTING in my room at twilight,
    In the last faint sunset's glow,
Watching the fast coming shadows
    Flitting softly to and fro.
Hushed is now all busy turmoil,
    Ended is the day of care,
And I, listening, wait the coming
    Of a footstep on the stair.

Hark ! I hear the firm tread sounding,
    Eagerly he comes to meet
One he knows awaits his coming,
    One who waits with welcome sweet.
Though to others I am humble,
    In his eyes I am most fair ;
Sweetest music to my hearing
    Is his footstep on the stair.

Lo, he comes ! Ah, when Life's over,
    And my days on earth are past,
When my heart, so strange and wayward,
    Shall be silent—calm at last,
Love dies not—my soul in Heaven,
    Though within that realm so fair,
Still will watch for you, my darling,
    Coming up the golden stair.

Lines,

I MET the friend I loved when but a child,
And as I clasped again his honest hand
And looked once more into his earnest eyes,
I was the happiest mortal in the land.
The long years sped since last I saw his face
Seemed but a dream—a dream most strange and wild,
For by his side the years seemed lifted up,
And I again a careless, happy child.
Yet pause I even now to note the change
The stamp of manhood shows upon his face,
While on my brow are lines of anxious care—
(The lot of all in Life's eventful race,)
    Yet O what joy! (and joys in life are few,)
    It is to see your face, O friend so true!

O cruel Time! to thus so quickly speed,
And leave your traces on our hearts and brows.
Relentless Time! that crushes out our youth,
Before whose power the mightiest mortal bows,
Yet, ah! you cannot touch the sacred Past,
Nor turn to blank Youth's written pages fair,
When Love was truth and Friendship not a name,
And Childhood built its " castles in the air."
So tarry by my side, beloved friend ;
Take once again my hand within your own,
And let me sit and look upon your face,
And listen to your voice's kindly tone.
    Friends of To-day, I do not doubt their truth,
    But, ah ! they cannot be the friends of youth.

Only a Tress of Hair,

ONLY a tress of soft dark hair,
　　And yet 'twill be,
Whatever fate this world may bring,
　　Most dear to me.

The head this tress adorned
　　Has laid in rest,
In true, confiding love,
　　Upon my breast.

The tress was severed then
　　That it might be,
A token dear from her, my friend,
　　Who so loved me.

Dark storms have crossed my path
　　Since last we met,
And yet her dear and loving face
　　I'll ne'er forget.

The sweet, low voice is silent now,
　　The head laid low,
And o'er her grave on yonder hill.
　　The flowers grow.

Time brought me many trials sore,
　　And heavy care,
And yet I fondly cherish still
　　Her tress of hair.

SENTIMENTAL.

The Omen.

TWO lovers sat watching one bright summer night,
 Hand in hand, cheek to cheek, the moon's beams,
Enjoying the present, the future unheeding,
 Their hearts all aglow with their own happy dreams.

The beautiful sky, by no cloudlet bedimmed,
 Strewn thickly with stars, was as blue
As the eye of the maiden, who dreamily pondered,
 And listened to promises seemingly true.

As they looked, two large stars in the heavens above
 Fixed their gaze. "That is mine," said the youth,
"As that star is my love ever constant and bright,
 As that star everlasting my truth."

"The other is mine. Brilliant omen of fate !"
 As she spoke blushes dyed her fair cheek,
The innocent thoughts to her lips found their way,
 And she spoke as love only can speak.

Long sat they thus gazing, all trouble forgetting—
 Not noting a cloud from afar,
Which drifting quite slowly but steadily gaining,
 Soon covered *his* clear, shining star.

That instant *her* star like a meteor flashed,
  It sparkled and fell to the ground,
Where it died—leaving vacant the place it had bright
  So now neither star could be found.

As trembling they saw the fair tokens departing,
  Grief arose in each heart, and with fears
Crowding backward the love with gloomy forebodings,
  They parted in sorrow and tears.

They met soon again but with faces averted,
  The love in *his* heart had grown cold ;
His vows were untrue and soon lightly were broken,
  As the cloud o'er his star had foretold.

She mingled in revelry, listened to praises,
  Her thoughts all the while away far.
With scorn on her lip and all murmurs disdaining
  She died—like her beautiful star.

Perhaps. .

"Since if you stood at my side to-day
  Only our hands would meet,
What matter if half the weary world
  Lies out between our feet."——PHŒBE CARY.

THE flower a hand has rudely pressed
  Will slowly droop and die,
A fallen star will ne'er more beam
  Within yon brilliant sky.
The tree that stood before the gale
  With proudly towering head,
At length the long continued storm
  Uproots from Earth's damp bed.

E'en so the love that firmly clung,
  With fervent faith and trust,
Unto the one whose cold neglect
  Slow crushed it to the dust.
Like as the tree, the sore tried heart
  At last will surely break,
And late repentance and kind words
  Dead love can never wake.

Perhaps the dog whose angry tooth
  Was buried in my hand,
I'll beckon with a gentle tone
  Again by me to stand.
Perhaps a little singing bird
  Who hears a serpent hiss,
At once does fly into its coils
  With joy and trustfulness.

E'en so, perhaps, in time my heart
  Will learn to love again,
And trust once more the treach'rous soul
  That bowed it low with pain.
Perhaps thy falseness I'll forget
  As years shall slow elapse.
I do not say thee, yea, or nay,
  I only say—Perhaps.

Parted.

WHEN the twilight's dusky mantle
    Turns to black the forests green,
When the world is calmly sleeping
    'Neath the bright moon's silvery beam,
When the nightwinds soft are wafting
    Flowers' pure incense to above,
All my soul is yearning toward thee,
    And I think of thee, my love.

As I wander o'er Life's pathway
  And my heart grows faint and lone,
And I weary turn from pleasure,
  Longing for thy voice and home,
Gentle Peace folds o'er my spirit
  Her soft pinions like a dove,
And my road seems far less lonely
  When I think of thee, my love.

Low thy graceful head is lying,   .
  O'er thy breast the daisies blow,
And the anguish of my bosom
  Only God and thou can know.
Though my bruised, rebellious spirit
  Dares to question Him above,
Still I strive to hush my murmurs
  When I think of thee, my love.

Do not enter at the portal !
  Tarry yet a while for me—
I am hastening up the pathway,
  Soon I'll stand again by thee.
Leave me not, beloved spirit,
  Wait beside the gate above—
Hand in hand once more *together*
  Let us enter in, my love.

Trials.

MANY the trials I meet in life
  As I hurry the journey along,
Many the trials, many the cares—
  And many a bitter wrong.

Many companions I dearly loved
  The Master has called away.
I know *they* watch and wait for me
  In the happy Far-away.

Often my fondly cherished hopes
    Are rudely dashed to earth,
And often friends I love the best
    I find are of little worth.

I wept o'er the loss of those I loved,
    I wept o'er my hopes' rude fall,
But the tears I shed when I found thee false
    Were the bitterest tears of all.

Many the trials I meet in life—
    They are waiting for great and small ;
But to find my trust in thee betrayed
    Is the heaviest trial of all.

Lines.

I AM sad and weary, darling,
    Lonely and sick at heart,
For I long for your dear presence
    Though we are so far apart.
O, to clasp your hand, my dear one,
    O, your kindly voice to hear.
Where-so-e'er your feet may wander,
    May God protect you, dear.

I shall watch for you returning,
    I can never love thee less,
May His watchful care be with you
    And your life forever bless.
Though long miles now stretch between us
    Yet in thought I'm ever near,
And my heart-felt prayer is ever
    That God will bless you, dear.

Ah ! be sure I'm thinking of you
　　Though your name I never speak,
And my heart is yearning toward you
　　With love thoughts true and deep.
Heaven guard my distant darling,
　　Be the skies above thee clear
From a single shade of clouding,
　　And may God protect you, dear.

Remember Me.

WHEN I am far away, dear one,
　　Yes, miles and miles from you, my friend,
May blessings hover o'er thy path,
　　And Fortune e'er thy steps attend.
My changeful life will often be
　　As turbid as a troubled sea,
Yet, O what joy 'twill be to know
　　That sometimes you will think of me.

Your honest love I do not doubt,
　　I clasp your warm and friendly hand,
I know no other truer friend
　　I'll ever find in any land,
God's blessings on your faithful heart.
　　Go where you will—where-e'er you be,
Let not time weaken Friendship's ties,
　　But, dearest one, remember me.

I know a future day will come,
　　A day when we shall meet again,
The joy of meeting will outweigh
　　By far the bitter parting pain.
Farewell ! your mem'ry, dear, will dwell
　　Within my heart on land or sea,
And may I never live to see
　　The day you have forgotten me.

Watching.

A SEA STORY.

SHE stood alone on the wild sea shore,
  Her lover was far away,
  Yet she watched and waited for his return
    Patiently day by day.
"'Tis many a day," I heard her say,
  " Since he sailed o'er the dark blue main,
But I'll murmur not, *he has not forgot,*
  I know he will come again."
O'er her brow so fair
  Her soft dark hair
Was tossed by the wind so wild,
  Yet her eyes so true
Scanned the Ocean's blue
  With the faith of a little child.
But no welcome mast
  Her vision passed
Though she watched with anxious pain,
  And whispered low:
" He will come, I know,
  Yes, he surely will come again."

The year passed by, her soft dark eye
  Grew dim with watching long,
Yet her heart's pure will was constant still,
  And her maiden love as strong ;
Yet she faded fast, and she died at last,
  Her watching all in vain.
From the distant strand, of a foreign land
  Her lover ne'er came again.
O'er her brow so calm
  The summer long
The roses bloom so pale,
  And the Robin's trill
And the Whip-poor-will
  Her early death bewail.
Yet I often dream, in the Twilight's gleam,
  I can hear her whisper low:
" I will murmur not, he has not forgot,
  He will come again, I know."

Discontent,

THEY come to greet me with their outstretched hands
   And bid me " welcome " in a hearty tone,
Yet in their midst my heart is discontent,
   And 'mong them all I feel but more alone.
Their voices cannot win my restless soul,
   Nor drive away the shades of lonely care,
I turn away from them unsatisfied
      Because you are not there.

What care I if they praise the songs I sing ?
   What matter if they doat upon my rhyme—
What matter if they crown me Pleasure's queen,
   If my heart is so lonely all the time ?
The crowd of smiling faces are to me
   As naught—although they beam so genial, fair—
I cannot meet and give them smile for smile,
      Because you are not there.

I'd rather see one honest face I love,
   And feel the touch of one beloved hand,
Whose clasp has power to thrill my icy heart
   Unmoved by merry strains from Flattery's band.
So, though they welcome me—a happy band—
   And jest with hearts so free from any care,
Among them all I feel but more alone
      Because you are not there.

• A Heart Song.

'TIS true that we are severed far,
　We ne'er may meet again, dear,
For I am here and you are there,
　And have been many a sad year.
My heart yearns ever to your own
　As flowers seek earliest morn's dew,
Yet still I never do repent
　That I have met and loved you.

My path in life comes never near
　The way you tread alone, dear.
You miss my presence by your side,
　And I, too, grieve you're not near,
Yet mem'ry sweet remains us both
　Of joys so pure we once knew,
My heart is better—tenderer,
　Since I have met and loved you.

Mine was a useless, dreary life,
　Without an end or aim, dear ;
Wrapped up in self I drew to me
　But scorn or pity—doubt—fear.
Since far from you I seek about
　To find what good I may do,
And live for others, not myself,
　Since I have met and loved you.

So, though we journey far apart
　And ne'er shall meet again, dear,
I'll pray for you and you for me
　With conscience from a blot clear.
And as I journey on and find
　'Mong many hearts, so few true,
My faith in human-kind dies not
　Since I have met and loved you.

God knoweth best—so don't complain,
　But bow unto His will, dear.
If meant that we should meet again
　He'll show the way to us clear.
But come what may, the world to me
　Is brighter, better, more true,
Than when I empty hearted roamed
　Before I met and loved you.

Drifting Apart,

DRIFTING apart! Drifting apart!
Our barks now float on Life's turbid tide,
But no longer gliding side by side,
And I miss thy voice of kindly cheer,
As I watch o'er the waste of waters drear,
　The masts of thy speeding bark.

　Drifting apart! Afar to roam,
And every rise of the billows' swell
Divides us further. Ah! is it well?
My soul says, nay—but so let it be—
I wave farewell, farewell to thee,
　And journey on alone.

　Drifting apart! Perhaps ere long
When my bark is lost fore'er from view,
When the storm clouds shroud the sky now blue,
When the tempest fills thy heart with fear,
You will long, too late, my voice to hear,
　And see thy course is wrong.

RELIGIOUS.

"Thy Will be Done,"

"THY will be done," O simple little words,
 And yet so hard for us to truly say;
To bow unquestioning before Thy will,
 And meekly bear the burdens of today.
Pity our weakness, O most holy Son!
 And teach our murmuring lips to say
   " Thy will be done."

" Thy will be done." See where the widow mourns,
 As o'er her dead companion sad tears fall,
Alone she stands—her heart's dear comrade gone,
 Nor answers to her wild despairing call.
O dry your eyes, poor mourner; think for him
 Has risen up Eternity's glad sun.
O may He help thy stricken soul to say
   " Thy will be done."

" Thy will be done." The mother weeping stands
 Beside the coffin of her cherished one;
The baby, snatched from off her loving breast
 Before its little life had scarce begun.
Beside her, Lord, in pitying kindness stand,
 And hold her hand, most gracious Holy one;
Thou know'st how hard for her poor lips to say
   " Thy will be done."

" Thy will be done." O how we need thy help
  To say those words with humble, trustful heart,
To bow before Thy will in everything,
  As in this weary world we take our part.
Thou knowest our weakness and how prone to stray,
  Rebellious, leaving all Thy work undone;
But Lord, forgive, and help us all to say
    " Thy will be done."

Have Trust in God.

HAVE trust in God,
  When o'er thy pathway heavy shadows lie,
When no kind friend nor earthly help is nigh
To cheer thy soul; when thy frail bark is driven
By darkest storms of life, look unto Heaven
            And trust in God.

  Have trust in God,
He knows the lonesome way is dark and drear,
He knows thy heart is often filled with fear;
But His strong hand is at the vessel's helm,
And though storms rave, they ne'er shall overwhelm,
            So trust in God.

  Have trust in God;
He bendeth low to hear thy faintest call,
He knoweth every trial—burden—all—
So when thy cares seem heaviest to bear,
Press on thy way with softly whispered prayer,
            And trust in God.

  Have trust in God,
And when thy bark shall breast the tide no more,
When life's long journey shall at last be o'er,
Then will thy soul, from its dark bondage free,
Soar to the heavenly shore and ever be
            Safe with its God.

Resignation.

HOW doth our minds e'er strive to see
   Into the dark futurity!
To pierce the gloom before our eyes,
The cloud that o'er the future lies,
And see our whole lives clear and plain,
How much of joy—how much of pain.
And often do we pass away
In longings vain the present day,
While fancy paints a scene more fair,
With flowers rich and scented air,
Which, by the contrast, dims the light
Of blessings that are now so bright.

Ah, foolish ones! to pass in scorn
The treasures of life's early morn,
To slight the jewels at our feet,
And grasp for those beyond our reach,
And for " What is to come " still sigh,
Until to-day has glided by !
O let us meet the coming years,
With all their pleasures, cares and fears.
Just as God's providence has planned,
And humbly take from His kind hand
The good, the ill, the toil, the rest,
E'er feeling that He knoweth best.

Submission.

MY heart doth not yet understand
   The workings of Thy wondrous hand,
      Nor know Thy righteous way;
But what is now as blackest night,
Thy mighty love will sometime light,
      Make plain some future day.

'Tis true the way looks lone and dark,
And often my faint, saddened heart
   Is filled with grief and pain ;
But when Thy gracious words I hear,
" Dear child, thy Lord is ever near,"
   The path seems bright again.

Then let me trust Thee more and more,
And when my weary days are o'er,
   And my bewildered sight
Shall look back over life again,
With all its mysteries made plain,
   I'll see that Thou wast right.

My Prayer,

HOLD Thou my hand,
  As o'er life's changing, stormy sea I float,
And storm-gusts fierce, threat oft to wreck my boat;
Oh ! when the billows roar and swell most high,
When naught I see but dark and frowning sky,
     Lord, near me stand.

     Lord, call to me
Whene'er with fancied strength I strive to guide,
Without Thy help, my bark across the tide ;
Oh, let not then Thy anger on me fall,
But deign the foolish wanderer to recall,
     Back unto Thee.

     Hold thou my hand,
And give me strength to battle boldly on ;
Ne'er shrinking, though the tide be swift and strong.
And when by yon bright shore my anchor's cast,
O, then with thankful soul may I at last
     Before Thee stand.

Be Thou My Guide.

I TREAD along life's changeful, rugged pathway,
   And gather often briers—sometimes flowers ;
Still, looking forth with hope in the to-morrow,
   I pass away Time's swiftly flying hours.
But naught of evil will my years betide,
If Thou, O Lord, wilt be my shield and guide.

Oft doth my heart, with sad and weary pining,
   Long for the coming of a brighter day,
And often to my thankless eyes discerning,
   Is naught but dreary darkness all the way.
And oft my lips with murmurings loud complain,
Because the blessings sent are mixed with pain.

Teach me, O Lord, with humble mind to praise Thee,
   Alike 'mid pleasure and in trouble sore ;
O, may I e'er, amidst life's stormiest billows,
   But cling unto and trust Thee more and more.
And lift my eyes in earnest faith above,
Relying on Thy strong, undying love.

Watch Thou o'er me through all the busy future,
   Within my soul in gracious kindness dwell,
And may I e'er amidst life's strangest changes,
   Still feel within myself, *Thou do'st all well.*
For naught but good can all my days betide,
If Thou, O Lord, wilt be my shield and guide.

www.ingramcontent.com/pod-product-compliance
Lightning Source LLC
Chambersburg PA
CBHW021423090426
42742CB00009B/1233